UNDER THE HOOD

THE HISTORY OF MUSTANGS

SETH HINGSTON

PowerKiDS press™

NEW YORK

Published in 2019 by The Rosen Publishing Group, Inc.
29 East 21st Street, New York, NY 10010

Editor: Elizabeth Krajnik
Book Design: Michael Flynn

Photo Credits: Cover (car) VanderWolf Images/Shutterstock.com; cover, p. 1 (emblem) Lerner Vadim/Shutterstock.com; cover, pp. 1, 3–4, 6–12, 14–22, 24–28, 30–32 (background) fotomck/Shutterstock.com; p. 5 Baranov E/Shutterstock.com; p. 7 Grzegorz Czapski/Shutterstock.com; pp. 7, 25 (orange Mustang) Barry Blackburn/Shutterstock.com; p. 8 John Olson/The LIFE Images Collection/Getty Images; p. 9 Caddy Man/Shutterstock.com; p. 11 Jewel Samad/AFP/Getty Images; p. 13 (GT4) David Rosenblum/Icon Sportswire/Getty Images; p. 13 (FR500C) https://commons.wikimedia.org/wiki/File:FordRacingMustangFR500C.jpg; p. 14 Pat Brollier/The Enthusiast Network/Getty Images; p. 15 action sports/Shutterstock.com; p. 16 FPG/Archive Photos/Getty Images; p. 17 Keith Bell/Shutterstock.com; p. 18 https://commons.wikimedia.org/wiki/File:%2778_Ford_Mustang_King_Cobra_(Sterling_Ford).jpg; p. 19 Steve Lagreca/Shutterstock.com; p. 21 National Motor Museum/Heritage Images/Hulton Archive/Getty Images; p. 23 Bill Pugliano/Getty Images; p. 25 (blue Mustang) https://commons.wikimedia.org/wiki/File:Wiki_gt_cs.jpg; pp. 26, 27 Eric Thayer/Getty Images; p. 29 Stefan Wermuth/Bloomberg/Getty Images; p. 30 wjarek/Shutterstock.com.

Library of Congress Cataloging-in-Publication Data

Names: Kingston, Seth, author.
Title: The history of Mustangs / Seth Kingston.
Description: New York : PowerKids Press, [2019] | Series: Under the hood | Includes index.
Identifiers: LCCN 2018031186| ISBN 9781538343401 (library bound) | ISBN 9781538344569 (pbk.) | ISBN 9781538344576 (6 pack)
Subjects: LCSH: Mustang automobile–History–Juvenile literature.
Classification: LCC TL215.M8 K56 2019 | DDC 629.222/2-dc23
LC record available at https://lccn.loc.gov/2018031186

Manufactured in the United States of America

CPSIA Compliance Information: Batch #CW19PK. For Further Information contact Rosen Publishing, New York, New York at 1-800-237-9932

CONTENTS

FORD MOTOR COMPANY

Ford is one of the most successful auto manufacturers in the United States. Henry Ford started the Ford Motor Company in 1903. The company began with 12 investors, or people who put money into a business with the goal of achieving a profit. On July 23, 1903, Ford sold its first car—the Ford Model A.

In 1913, Ford introduced the assembly line to auto production. It was the first company to do so. An assembly line is a system of machines and workers in which work passes down the line step by step until the product is completed. The assembly line made making cars faster and easier.

Today, almost all cars are made on assembly lines. Ford focuses on **innovation** with **design** and **technology**. One of the company's greatest creations is the Mustang.

THE ASSEMBLY LINE MADE IT POSSIBLE TO BUILD A MODEL T IN JUST 1.5 HOURS. BEFORE THE ASSEMBLY LINE, IT TOOK ABOUT 12.5 HOURS. THIS ALSO HELPED KEEP THE PRICE OF THE MODEL T LOW.

THE MODEL T

One of Ford's most notable cars was the Model T, which the company first made in 1908. Before the Model T, most cars were luxury goods and only wealthy people could afford them. The Model T was the first car made to be affordable and **reliable**. The Model T was in production until 1927, and about 15 million were sold!

WHAT'S A PONY CAR?

The Ford Mustang was the first pony car. A pony car is a smaller two-door car with sporty styling and high performance. Pony cars are less expensive than many European sports cars. These cars are also different from most European sports cars because they are less **exclusive**. Mustangs have seats in the back, while most other sports cars only have two seats.

On April 17, 1964, Ford introduced the Mustang at the New York World's Fair. Ford hoped to sell 100,000 Mustangs in the first year. The company sold 22,000 Mustangs in the first day! In the car's first 18 months, Ford sold 1 million Mustangs. The Mustang is one of the fastest-selling cars in history. They still sell well: in the first five months of 2018, Ford sold 35,028 Mustangs.

OTHER PONY CARS INCLUDE THE PONTIAC FIREBIRD, THE CHEVROLET CAMARO, THE PLYMOUTH BARRACUDA, AND THE DODGE CHALLENGER.

START YOUR ENGINES

A MUSTANG SERVED AS THE PACE CAR FOR THE 1964 INDIANAPOLIS 500. THIS BOOSTED THE CAR'S SUCCESS. ANOTHER REASON PEOPLE WANTED TO BUY MUSTANGS IS BECAUSE THE CARS APPEARED IN A NUMBER OF MOVIES.

1965 MUSTANG GT 350

1967 CHEVROLET CAMARO

COMPETING WITH EUROPEAN COMPANIES

Before Ford introduced the Mustang, European companies such as Alfa Romeo, Ferrari, and Lamborghini were the main producers of sports cars. However, the sports car game changed when two Ford employees, Lee Iacocca and Donald Frey, came up with the idea of a pony car. They decided the new Ford sports car would need to have a back seat. Adding a back seat may seem simple today, but at the time no other company had done that.

LEE IACOCCA

WHEN THE MUSTANG MADE ITS DEBUT, OR FIRST APPEARANCE, IT COST JUST $2,368. IN TODAY'S MONEY, THAT WOULD BE $19,218. THE LEAST EXPENSIVE 2019 MUSTANG COSTS $25,845.

The Mustang's back seat and large trunk made it much more practical than European sports cars. It had enough space for a small family and their luggage. By 1967, many other American auto manufacturers, including Chevrolet and Pontiac, had their own **versions** of a pony car.

CUSTOMIZING YOUR MUSTANG

From the beginning, the Mustang has been customizable, which means that customers can choose between options, or choices, such as which color they want or whether they want a convertible or a coupe, or hardtop. Some Mustang coupes are called fastbacks.

As of 2018, Ford offered eight Mustang models: the Ecoboost Fastback and Convertible, the Ecoboost Premium Fastback and Convertible, the GT Fastback, the GT Premium Fastback and Convertible, and the Bullitt. Each model has many different options, including paint color, inside color, safety packages, performance packages, and engine size.

Most **passenger** cars have fewer than six **cylinders**. However, modern Mustangs have either a V-6 or V-8 engine. The original Mustang had a V-6 engine, but starting in 1968, some Mustang models were offered with a V-8 engine.

START YOUR ENGINES

A V-6 OR V-8 ENGINE IS AN ENGINE THAT HAS SIX OR EIGHT CYLINDERS ARRANGED IN A "V" SHAPE. THE MORE CYLINDERS AN ENGINE HAS, THE MORE POWERFUL IT IS.

A BASIC 2019 MUSTANG BULLITT COSTS $46,595. THE CAR HAS A 5.0-LITER V-8 ENGINE AND IS ONLY AVAILABLE AS A FASTBACK.

MAKING TURNKEY RACECARS

Racecars aren't meant to be driven on regular roads. They're often more powerful and have special parts to keep the driver safe. Most racecars only have a seat for the driver. Car manufacturers like to make racecars to showcase their cars' speed and power and the company's design and **engineering** abilities.

As of 2018, Ford makes two kinds of turnkey racecars. These cars are called turnkey racecars because they can be driven in races without changes to the body or the engine. Drivers just need to turn the key. The Ford Mustang GT4, which is based on the Ford Shelby GT350R-C, competes in sports car championships such as the Pirelli World Challenge GTS/GT4 series. The Ford Mustang FP350S competes in the Trans Am and SCCA racing classes.

THE MUSTANG FP350S STARTS AT $114,990. THE GT4 STARTS AT $225,000.

THE MUSTANG FR500C

One of Ford's most successful turnkey racecars was the Mustang FR500C. This Mustang had a 5.0-liter, 400-horsepower engine and cost $125,000. Multimatic, an engineering company, built the Mustang FR500C for customers competing in the Grand-Am Cup series and other international racing series. It was nicknamed the Boy Racer. The Mustang FR500C won the Grand-Am drivers', manufacturers', and team championships in 2005, 2008, and 2009.

MUSTANG GT4

MUSTANGS IN RACING

For a stretch of time in the 1950s and 1960s, American automakers didn't take part in auto racing because of a ban put in place by the Automobile Manufacturers Association. However, Ford announced it would start racing again in 1962—just in time for the Mustang to debut.

SOME NATIONAL HOT ROD ASSOCIATION (NHRA) TEAMS RACE MUSTANGS. HOT RODS ARE CARS THAT ARE REBUILT OR CHANGED TO BE FASTER. THE NHRA IS A DRAG-RACING ORGANIZATION.

The Mustang made its racing debut in the 1964 Tour de France **rally**. Mustangs took first and second place in their class. The Mustang made its American debut in drag racing. In drag racing, cars race next to each other in a straight line.

Mustangs have also raced in National Association for Stock Car Auto Racing (NASCAR) races. A stock car is a racecar that's based on an existing production car. In NASCAR races, cars race on an oval-shaped track. NASCAR is the most popular racing series in the United States.

FIRST GENERATION 1965–1973

The first generation of Mustangs debuted in 1964, but these cars were sold as 1965 models. The cars built between April and August 1964 are often called 1964½ Mustangs, but they belong to the 1965 model year. However, these Mustangs were different from the other 1965 models. They had a different electrical system and a smaller V-8 engine that produced less horsepower. Only 121,538 of these 1964½ models were produced.

The 1964½ Mustang had many different options. It could have a six-cylinder or V-8 engine. It could have 101 horsepower in the six-cylinder engine or 164 horsepower or 210 horsepower in the V-8 engines. Customers could choose what type of **transmission** they wanted. The 1964½ came in a convertible or a coupe.

IN 1967, FORD REDESIGNED THE MUSTANG. IT BECAME BIGGER AND GOT A BIGGER ENGINE—A 6.4-LITER V-8 THAT PRODUCED 320 HORSEPOWER.

SECOND GENERATION 1974–1978

Ford marketed the second-generation Mustang as the Ford Mustang II. This model was introduced at a turning point in the car manufacturing industry. In response to the changing times, Ford redesigned the Mustang. The Mustang II was based on the design of the Ford Pinto. The second generation only came as a hatchback or coupe.

THE MUSTANG II CAME IN A NUMBER OF DIFFERENT PACKAGES. THE COBRA II, PICTURED HERE, WAS A RACE-INSPIRED CAR WITH DIFFERENT BODY PARTS THAT MADE IT STAND OUT FROM THE OTHER MODELS.

In the first year, the Mustang II only had the option of a four-cylinder, 92-horsepower engine or a V-6, 105-horsepower engine. In 1975, Ford reintroduced the option of a V-8 engine. The engine also came in two sizes, 2.3 liters or 2.8 liters. The Mustang still wasn't as powerful as other sports cars at the time and had a top speed of only 99 miles (159.3 km) per hour.

1977 MUSTANG II

THIRD GENERATION 1979–1993

The 1979 Mustang was larger than previous models. It was built on Ford's Fox platform, or frame, and is often called the Fox or Fox Body Mustang. It looked more like European sports cars and less like the previous generations of Mustangs. It was also much lighter than the Mustang II.

The Fox Body Mustang had a new running horse logo and four headlights. It was also only available as a coupe or a hatchback. The 1979 model was available with a 2.3-liter four-cylinder engine, a 2.8-liter V-6, a 3.3-liter six-cylinder, or a 5.0-liter V-8 engine.

The third-generation Mustang was more popular than the second-generation Mustang. In 1983, Ford reintroduced the option of a convertible top on the Mustang. There were also other changes, such as a rounder nose.

IN 1987, THE FOX BODY WAS REDESIGNED TO HAVE MORE **AERODYNAMIC** HEADLIGHTS, A SMOOTHER NOSE, AND BLACK EXTERIOR MOLDINGS. IT WAS ALSO AVAILABLE WITH A 2.3-LITER FOUR-CYLINDER OR 5.0-LITER V-8 ENGINE.

THE MUSTANG SVO

In 1984, Ford introduced the Mustang SVO. The SVO was a special-**edition** model. Only 4,508 SVOs were produced. The SVO had a turbo four-cylinder engine that produced 175 horsepower. It had a top speed of almost 135 miles (217 km) per hour and could go from 0 to 60 miles (0 to 96.6 km) per hour in just 7.5 seconds. At the time, it was the fastest Mustang available. However, the SVO was the most expensive Mustang ever made, and because of this, it didn't sell very well.

START YOUR ENGINES

THE 1979 MUSTANG WAS CHOSEN AS THE PACE CAR FOR THAT YEAR'S INDIANAPOLIS 500. TO CELEBRATE, FORD PRODUCED 11,000 "OFFICIAL PACE CAR" HATCHBACKS.

FOURTH GENERATION 1994–2004

In 1994, the Mustang celebrated its 30th anniversary with the debut of its fourth generation. After 14 years, Ford retired the Fox Body and came up with a new design. Ford got rid of the hatchback option, but convertibles and coupes were still available. The 1994 Mustang had a 3.8-liter, V-6 engine that produced 145 horsepower.

Ford redesigned the Mustang again for its 35th anniversary in 1999. The new Mustang had sharper lines, larger wheel arches, and a more powerful engine with 190 horsepower. Ford produced 4,628 limited-edition Mustang GTs to celebrate.

In 2004, Ford produced a 40th anniversary edition of the Mustang. This car was available in coupe and convertible options of the standard and GT models. The package included special exterior and interior changes.

IN 2003, FORD PRODUCED ITS 300 MILLIONTH CAR, A RED 2004 MUSTANG GT CONVERTIBLE.

THE BULLITT

In 2001, Ford launched the Bullitt, a new special-edition Mustang. The Bullitt was based on the 2001 Mustang GT but had some parts that looked more like earlier Mustang models. The Bullitt only came in three colors: Dark Highland Green, True Blue, and Black. It was only available as a coupe and just 5,582 Bullitts were produced. Ford released other editions of the Bullitt in 2008 and 2019.

FIFTH GENERATION 2005–2014

The fifth-generation Mustangs were designed to be faster and more powerful than previous generations. The car's styling looked more like that of the older generations of Mustangs and less like the fourth generation. The fifth generation got a new 4.0-liter V-6 engine that produced 210 horsepower. It was available as a coupe or a convertible.

In 2011, Ford reintroduced the Mustang Boss 302. The original Mustang Boss was made in 1979 and 1980. The 2012 Boss 302 was low to the ground and very aerodynamic. It had a V-8 engine that produced 444 horsepower. The Boss could go from 0 to 60 miles (0 to 96.6 km) per hour in 4.3 seconds and had a top speed of 155 miles (249.5 km) per hour.

IN 2006, FORD INTRODUCED THE MUSTANG GT/CS, WHICH STANDS FOR CALIFORNIA SPECIAL. THE ORIGINAL CALIFORNIA SPECIAL MUSTANG WAS MADE IN 1968. THE MUSTANG GT/CS LOOKED SIMILAR TO THE 2007–2008 SHELBY GT.

GT/CS

VIRGINIA
DONT TREAD ON ME
GT/CS

SIXTH GENERATION
2015–PRESENT

The sixth-generation Mustang marks the 50th anniversary of Mustang production. Ford used design elements from early Mustangs in a modern way to keep the sixth generation stylish. One of these elements is the return of the fastback. The sixth-generation Mustang is longer, lower, and wider than the fifth-generation Mustang. There are three engine options for the sixth-generation Mustangs: a 2.3-liter four-cylinder, a 3.7-liter V-6, and a 5.0-liter V-8.

TO CELEBRATE MUSTANG'S 50TH ANNIVERSARY, FORD CREATED A SPECIAL EDITION OF THE 2015 MUSTANG. THERE WERE 1,964 MUSTANG 50-YEAR EDITIONS PRODUCED.

Like other generations before it, the sixth-generation Mustang is highly customizable. According to Ford, one of its goals is to allow the customer to keep their Mustang more affordable or make it as flashy as they like. There are different interior options, wheel combinations, performance features, and sound system options.

THE SUCCESS OF MUSTANGS

The pony car was designed to be an affordable, customizable sports car for the average American car lover. Upon its introduction, the Mustang was an immediate success and it remains a success today. Mustangs are one of the most popular American sports cars.

Through the years, some Mustang generations have sold better than others. Ford sold the most Mustangs in 1966 with 607,500 cars. Today, the Mustang competes for sales with cars like the Chevrolet Camaro and the Dodge Challenger.

If you decide to buy a Mustang one day, you'll have a number of models to choose from. Once you pick which model you want, you can then pick the color, roof type, hood, headlights, and much more. People like having all of these options because they get to make their Mustangs exactly how they want them.

FORD IS SAID TO BE MOVING UP PRODUCTION OF THE SEVENTH-GENERATION MUSTANG FROM 2022 TO 2020. DO YOU THINK THE SEVENTH-GENERATION MUSTANG WILL LOOK SIMILAR TO THE SIXTH-GENERATION MUSTANG?

TIMELINE

1903 › Henry Ford starts the Ford Motor Company.

1908 › Ford releases the Model T.

1913 › Ford introduces the assembly line to auto production.

April 17, 1964 › Ford introduces the Mustang at the New York World's Fair. The first generation is produced until 1973.

1974 › Ford releases the second-generation Mustang.

1979 › Ford releases the third-generation Mustang.

1994 › Ford releases the fourth-generation Mustang.

2005 › Ford releases the fifth-generation Mustang.

2015 › Ford releases the sixth-generation Mustang.

GLOSSARY

aerodynamic: The qualities of an object that affect how easily it's able to move through the air.

cylinder: A tube-shaped part of an engine where power is created.

design: The way something has been made. Also, to create the plan for something.

edition: One of the forms in which something is presented.

engineering: The study and practice of using math and science to do useful things, such as building machines.

exclusive: Available to only a few people, often because of high cost.

innovation: A new way of doing things.

passenger: Someone riding on or in a vehicle.

rally: A type of automobile race using regular roads and traffic rules in which the drivers have to keep an average speed between checkpoints over an unknown route.

reliable: Dependable.

technology: The way people do something and the tools they use.

transmission: The part of a car or another vehicle that uses the engine's power to turn the wheels.

version: A form of something that is different from the ones that came before it.

INDEX

WEBSITES

Due to the changing nature of Internet links, PowerKids Press has developed an online list of websites related to the subject of this book. This site is updated regularly. Please use this link to access the list: www.powerkidslinks.com/hood/mustangs